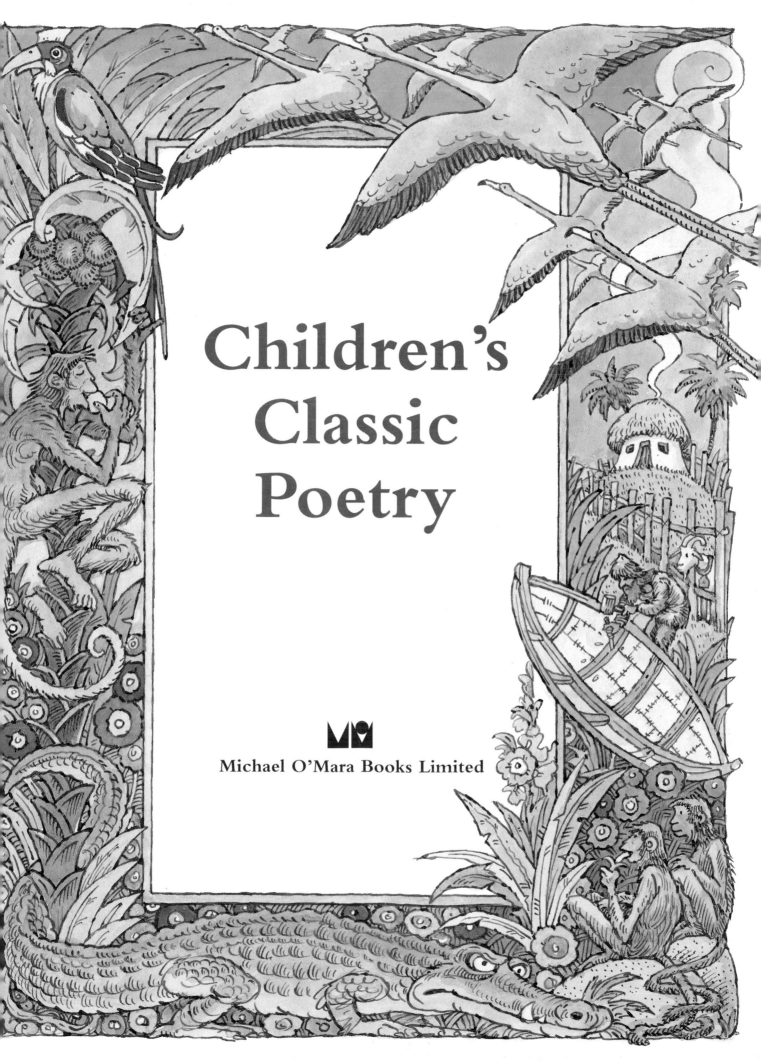

Children's Classic Poetry

Michael O'Mara Books Limited

This selection first published in Great Britain in 1998 by
Michael O'Mara Books Limited, 9 Lion Yard,
Tremadoc Road, London SW4 7NQ

This selection © 1998 Michael O'Mara Books
Illustrations © 1998 Robin Lawrie

Typeset by Florencetype, Devon
Text design by Reo Design Partnership
Poetry selection by Helen Burnford
Poetry editor Mike Freeman

ISBN 1-85479-355-1

Printed and bound in Singapore by Tien Wah Press.

Acknowledgments

The publishers gratefully acknowledge permission to reproduce the following
copyright material.

(UK & Commonwealth) 'The King's Breakfast' by A.A. Milne, reprinted by
permission of Methuen Children's Books (a division of Reed International Books Ltd.)

(US) 'The King's Breakfast' by A.A. Milne, from *When We Were Very Young* by
A.A. Milne. Copyright 1924 by E.P. Dutton, renewed 1952 by A.A. Milne. Used by
permission of Dutton Children's Books, a division of Penguin Putnam Inc.

'A Smuggler's Song' by Rudyard Kipling, from *The Definitive Edition of Rudyard
Kipling's Verse*. Reprinted by permission of A.P. Watt Ltd on behalf of
The National Trust.

'Waltzing Matilda' by Marie Cowan and A. B. Paterson
Copyright © 1936 by Allan & Co., Prop. Ltd.
Copyright © 1941 by Carl Fischer, Inc.
Copyrights renewed. All rights reserved. Reprinted by permission.

'Weathers' and 'Snow in the Suburbs' by Thomas Hardy, from *The Complete Poems
of Thomas Hardy* edited by James Gibson. Reprinted by permission of Papermac.

Contents

Love and Beauty

Laughter and Tears

People and Places

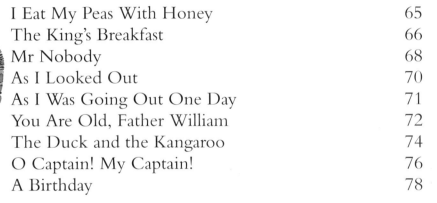

Birds and Beasts

I Had a Little Pony

I had a little pony,
　　His name was Dapple-gray,
I lent him to a lady,
　　To ride a mile away;
She whipped him, she slashed him,
　　She rode him through the mire;
I would not lend my pony now
　　For all the lady's hire.

Anon

The Tiger

Tiger, tiger, burning bright
In the forests of the night,
What immortal hand or eye
Could frame thy fearful symmetry?

In what distant deeps or skies
Burnt the fire of thine eyes?
On what wings dare he aspire?
What the hand dare seize the fire?

And what shoulder and what art
Could twist the sinews of thy heart?
And, when thy heart began to beat,
What dread hand? and what dread feet?

What the hammer? What the chain?
In what furnace was thy brain?
What the anvil? What dread grasp
Dare its deadly terrors clasp?

When the stars threw down their spears,
And watered heaven with their tears,
Did he smile his work to see?
Did he who made the lamb make thee?

Tiger, tiger, burning bright
In the forests of the night,
What immortal hand or eye
Dare frame thy fearful symmetry?

William Blake 1757–1827

How Doth
the Little Crocodile

How doth the little crocodile
Improve his shining tail;
And pour the waters of the Nile
On every golden scale!

How cheerfully he seems to grin,
How neatly spreads his claws,
And welcomes little fishes in,
With gently smiling jaws!
Lewis Carroll 1832–1898

Mary Had a
Crocodile

Mary had a crocodile
That ate a child each day;
But interfering people came
And took her pet away.
Anon

The Cow

The friendly cow, all red and white,
I love with all my heart:
She gives me cream with all her might,
To eat with apple-tart.

She wanders lowing here and there,
And yet she cannot stray,
All in the pleasant open air,
The pleasant light of day;

And blown by all the winds that pass
And wet with all the showers,
She walks among the meadow grass
And eats the meadow flowers.
                    Robert Louis Stevenson 1850−1894

from The Kitten and the Falling Leaves

See the Kitten on the wall,
Sporting with the leaves that fall,
Withered leaves – one-two-and three –
From the lofty elder-tree!
Through the calm and frosty air
Of this morning bright and fair,
Eddying round and round they sink
Softly, slowly: one might think,
From the motions that are made,
Every little leaf conveyed
Sylph or Faery hither tending,
To this lower world descending,
Each invisible and mute
In his wavering parachute.

– But the Kitten, how she starts,
Crouches, stretches, paws, and darts!
First at one, and then its fellow
Just as light and just as yellow.
There are many now – now one –
Now they stop and there are none:

What intenseness of desire
In her upward eye of fire!
With a tiger-leap half-way
Now she meets the coming prey,
Lets it go as fast, and then
Has it in her power again:
Now she works with three or four,
Like an Indian conjurer;
Quick as he in feats of art,
Far beyond in joy of heart.

Were her antics played in the eye
Of a thousand standers-by,
Clapping hands with shout and stare,
What would little Tabby care
For the plaudits of the crowd?
William Wordsworth 1770 – 1850

11

The Parrot

Within her gilded cage confined,
I saw a dazzling Belle,
A Parrot of that famous kind
Whose name is NON-PAREIL.

Like beads of glossy jet her eyes;
And, smoothed by Nature's skill,
With pearl or gleaming agate vies
Her finely-curvèd bill.

Her plumy mantle's living hues
In mass opposed to mass,
Outshine the splendour that imbues
The robes of pictured glass.

And, sooth to say, an apter Mate
Did never tempt the choice
Of feathered Thing most delicate
In figure and in voice.

But, exiled from Australian bowers,
And singleness her lot,
She trills her song with tutored powers,
Or mocks each casual note.

No more of pity for regrets
With which she may have striven!
Now but in wantonness she frets,
Or spite, if cause be given.

Arch, volatile, a sportive bird
By social glee inspired;
Ambitious to be seen or heard,
And pleased to be admired!
William Wordsworth 1770 – 1850

from
Birds of Paradise

Golden-winged, silver-winged,
   Winged with flashing flame,
Such a flight of birds I saw,
   Birds without a name:
Singing songs in their own tongue –
   Song of songs – they came.

One to another calling,
   Each answering each,
One to another calling
   In their proper speech:
High above my head they wheeled,
   Far out of reach.

14

On wings of flame they went and came
  With a cadenced clang:
  Their silver wings tinkled,
  Their golden wings rang;
The wind it whistled through their wings
  Where in heaven they sang.

  They flashed and they darted
  Awhile before mine eyes,
Mounting, mounting, mounting still,
  In haste to scale the skies,
Birds without a nest on earth,
  Birds of Paradise.
        Christina Rossetti 1830 – 1894

Coyote

Blown out of the prairie in twilight and dew,
Half bold and half timid, yet lazy all through;
Loth ever to leave, and yet fearful to stay,
He limps in the clearing, an outcast in grey.

A shade on the stubble, a ghost by the wall,
Now leaping, now limping, now risking a fall,
Lop-eared and large-jointed, but ever alway
A thoroughly vagabond outcast in grey.

Here, Carlo, old fellow, he's one of your kind,
Go seek him, and bring him in out of the wind.
What! snarling, my Carlo! So – even dogs may
Deny their own kin in the outcast in grey.

Well, take what you will, though it be on the sly,
Marauding or begging, I shall not ask why;
But will call it a dole, just to help on his way
A four-footed friar in orders of grey!

Bret Harte 1836 –1902

The Woodman's Dog

Shaggy, and lean, and shrewd, with pointed ears
And tail cropped short, half lurcher and half cur –
His dog attends him. Close behind his heel
Now creeps he slow; and now with many a frisk
Wild-scampering, snatches up the drifted snow
With ivory teeth, or plows it with his snout;
Then shakes his powdered coat and barks for joy.

William Cowper 1731–1800

Mary's Lamb

Mary had a little lamb,
Its fleece was white as snow,
And everywhere that Mary went
The lamb was sure to go;
He followed her to school one day –
That was against the rule,
It made the children laugh and play
To see a lamb at school.

And so the teacher turned him out,
But still he lingered near,
And waited patiently about,
Till Mary did appear.
And then he ran to her and laid
His head upon her arm,
As if he said, 'I'm not afraid –
You'll shield me from all harm.'

'What makes the lamb love Mary so?'
The little children cry;
'Oh, Mary loves the lamb, you know,'
The teacher did reply,
'And you each gentle animal
In confidence may bind,
And make it follow at your call,
If you are always kind.'

Sarah Josepha Hale 1788–1879

There was a Monkey

There was a monkey climbed a tree,
When he fell down, then down fell he.

There was a crow sat on a stone,
When he was gone, then there was none.

There was an old wife did eat an apple,
When she ate two, she ate a couple.

There was a horse going to the mill,
When he went on, he stood not still.

There was a butcher cut his thumb,
When it did bleed, then blood did come.

There was a lackey ran a race,
When he ran fast, he ran apace.

There was a cobbler clouting shoon,
When they were mended, they were done.

There was a navy went to Spain,
When it returned it came again.

Anon

Wind and Weather

Whether the Weather Be Fine

Whether the weather be fine
Or whether the weather be not,
Whether the weather be cold
Or whether the weather be hot,
We'll weather the weather
Whatever the weather,
Whether we like it or not.

Anon

Spring and Fall

to a young child

Margaret, are you grieving
Over Goldengrove unleaving?
Leaves, like the things of man, you
With your fresh thoughts care for, can you?
Ah! as the heart grows older
It will come to such sights colder
By and by, nor spare a sigh
Though worlds of wanwood leafmeal lie;
And yet you *will* weep and know why.
Now no matter, child, the name:
Sorrow's springs are the same.
Nor mouth had, no nor mind, expressed
What heart heard of, ghost guessed:
It is the blight man was born for,
It is Margaret you mourn for.
Gerard Manley Hopkins 1844 – 1889

Weathers

This is the weather the cuckoo likes,
    And so do I;
When showers betumble the chestnut spikes,
    And nestlings fly:
And the little brown nightingale bills his best,
And they sit outside at "The Travellers' Rest",
And maids come forth sprig-muslin drest,
And citizens dream of the south and west,
    And so do I.

This is the weather the shepherd shuns,
    And so do I;
When beeches drip in browns and duns,
    And thresh, and ply;
And hill-hid tides throb, throe on throe,
And meadow rivulets overflow,
And drops on gate-bars hang in a row,
And rooks in families homeward go,
    And so do I.

Thomas Hardy 1840 – 1928

The North Wind
Doth Blow

The north wind doth blow
And we shall have snow,
And what will poor robin do then, poor thing?
  He'll sit in a barn,
    And keep himself warm,
And hide his head under his wing, poor thing!

The north wind doth blow
And we shall have snow,
And what will the dormouse do then, poor thing?
    Roll'd up like a ball,
    In his nest snug and small,
He'll sleep till warm weather comes in, poor thing!

The north wind doth blow
And we shall have snow,
And what will the children do then, poor things?
    When lessons are done,
    They must skip, jump, and run,
Until they have made themselves warm, poor things!

Anon

Snow

In the gloom of whiteness,
In the great silence of snow,
A child was sighing
And bitterly saying: 'Oh,
They have killed a white bird up there on her nest,
The down is fluttering from her breast!'
And still it fell through the dusky brightness
On the child crying for the bird of the snow.

Edward Thomas 1878–1917

Snow in the Suburbs

Every branch big with it,
Bent every twig with it;
Every fork like a white web-foot;
Every street and pavement mute:
Some flakes have lost their way, and grope back
    upward, when
Meeting those meandering down they turn and
    descend again.
The palings are glued together like a wall,
And there is no waft of wind with the fleecy fall.

A sparrow enters the tree,
Whereon immediately
A snow-lump thrice his own slight size
Descends on him and showers his head and eyes,
And overturns him,
And near inurns him,
And lights on a nether twig, when its brush
Starts off a volley of other lodging lumps with a rush.

The steps are a blanched slope,
Up which, with feeble hope,
A black cat comes, wide-eyed and thin;
And we take him in.

Thomas Hardy 1840 –1928

The Echoing Green

The sun does arise,
And make happy the skies;
The merry bells ring
To welcome the spring;
The skylark and thrush,
The birds of the bush,
Sing louder around
To the bells' cheerful sound,
While our sports shall be seen
On the Echoing Green.

Old John, with white hair,
Does laugh away care,
Sitting under the oak,
Among the old folk.
They laugh at our play,
And soon they all say:
'Such, such were the joys
When we all, girls and boys,
In our youth-time were seen
On the Echoing Green.'

Till the little ones, weary,
No more can be merry;
The sun does descend,
And our sports have an end.
Round the laps of their mothers
Many sisters and brothers,
Like birds in their nest,
Are ready for rest,
And sport no more seen
On the darkening Green.
            William Blake
            1757–1827

Rain

More than the wind, more than the snow,
More than the sunshine, I love rain;
Whether it droppeth soft and low
Whether it rusheth amain.

Dark as the night it spreadeth its wings,
Slow and silently up on the hills;
Then sweeps o'er the vale, like a steed that springs
From the grasp of a thousand wills.

Swift sweeps under heaven the raven cloud's flight;
And the land and the lakes and the main
Lie belted beneath with steel-bright light,
The light of the swift-rushing rain.

On evenings of summer, when sunlight is low,
Soft the rain falls from opal-hued skies;
And the flowers the most delicate summer can show
Are not stirr'd by its gentle surprise.

It falls on the pools, and no wrinkling it makes,
But touching melts in, like the smile
That sinks in the face of a dreamer, but breaks
Not the calm of his dream's happy wile.

The grass rises up as it falls on the meads,
The bird softlier sings in his bower,
And the circles of gnats circle on like wing'd seeds
Through the soft sunny lines of the shower.

Ebenezer Jones 1820 – 1860

Windy Nights

Whenever the moon and stars are set,
   Whenever the wind is high,
All night long in the dark and wet,
   A man goes riding by.
Late in the night when the fires are out,
Why does he gallop and gallop about?

Whenever the trees are crying aloud,
   And ships are tossed at sea,
By, on the highway, low and loud,
   By at the gallop goes he.
By at the gallop he goes, and then
By he comes back at the gallop again.
     Robert Louis Stevenson 1850 – 1894

Rain in Summer

How beautiful is the rain!
After the dust and heat,
In the broad and fiery street,
In the narrow lane,
How beautiful is the rain!

How it clatters along the roofs,
Like the tramp of hoofs!
How it gushes and struggles out
From the throat of the overflowing spout!
Across the window pane
It pours and pours;
And swift and wide,
With a muddy tide,
Like a river down the gutter roars
The rain, the welcome rain!
Henry Wadsworth Longfellow 1807–1882

Mystery and Magic

A Cornish Charm

From Ghosties and Ghoulies
And long-leggity Beasties,
And all things that go BUMP
in the night –
Good Lord, deliver us!

Anon

The Riddling Knight

There were three sisters fair and bright,
  Jennifer, Gentle, and Rosemary,
And they three loved one valiant knight –
  As the dow flies over the mulberry-tree.

The eldest sister let him in,
And barr'd the door with a silver pin.

The second sister made his bed,
And placed soft pillows under his head.

The youngest sister that same night
Was resolved for to wed wi' this valiant knight.

'And if you can answer questions three,
O then, fair maid, I'll marry wi' thee.

'O what is louder nor a horn,
Or what is sharper nor a thorn?

'Or what is heavier nor the lead,
Or what is better nor the bread?

'Or what is longer nor the way,
Or what is deeper nor the sea?'

'O shame is louder nor a horn,
And hunger is sharper nor a thorn.

'O sin is heavier nor the lead,
The blessing's better nor the bread.

'O the wind is longer nor the way
And love is deeper nor the sea.'

'You have answer'd aright my questions three,'
  Jennifer, Gentle, and Rosemary;
'And now, fair maid, I'll marry wi' thee,'
  As the dow flies over the mulberry-tree.

  Anon

Jabberwocky

'Twas brillig, and the slithy toves
Did gyre and gimble in the wabe:
All mimsy were the borogoves,
And the mome raths outgrabe.

"Beware the Jabberwock, my son!
The jaws that bite, the claws that catch!
Beware the Jubjub bird, and shun
The frumious Bandersnatch!"

He took his vorpal sword in hand:
Long time the manxome foe he sought –
So rested he by the Tumtum tree,
And stood awhile in thought.

And, as in uffish thought he stood,
The Jabberwock, with eyes of flame,
Came whiffling through the tulgey wood,
And burbled as it came!

One, two! One, two! And through and through
The vorpal blade went snicker-snack!
He left it dead, and with its head
He went galumphing back.

"And hast thou slain the Jabberwock?
Come to my arms, my beamish boy!
O frabjous day! Callooh! Callay!"
He chortled in his joy.

'Twas brillig, and the slithy toves
Did gyre and gimble in the wabe:
All mimsy were the borogoves,
And the mome raths outgrabe.

Lewis Carroll 1832–1898

Kubla Khan

In Xanadu did Kubla Khan
   A stately pleasure-dome decree:
Where Alph, the sacred river, ran
Through caverns measureless to man
   Down to a sunless sea.
So twice five miles of fertile ground
With walls and tower were girdled round:
And there were gardens bright with sinuous rills
Where blossom'd many an incense-bearing tree;
And here were forests ancient as the hills,
Enfolding sunny spots of greenery.

But O, that deep romantic chasm which slanted
Down the green hill athwart a cedarn cover!
A savage place! as holy and enchanted
As e'er beneath a waning moon was haunted
By woman wailing for her demon-lover!
And from this chasm, with ceaseless turmoil seething,
As if this earth in fast thick pants were breathing,
A mighty fountain momently was forced;
Amid whose swift half-intermitted burst
Huge fragments vaulted like rebounding hail,
Or chaffy grain beneath the thresher's flail:
And 'mid these dancing rocks at once and ever
It flung up momently the sacred river.
Five miles meandering with a mazy motion
Through wood and dale the sacred river ran,
Then reach'd the caverns measureless to man,
And sank in tumult to a lifeless ocean:
And 'mid this tumult Kubla heard from far
Ancestral voices prophesying war!

The shadow of the dome of pleasure
Floated midway on the waves;
Where was heard the mingled measure
From the fountain and the caves.
It was a miracle of rare device,
A sunny pleasure-dome with caves
        of ice!

A damsel with a dulcimer
In a vision once I saw:
It was an Abyssinian maid,
And on her dulcimer she play'd,
Singing of Mount Abora.
Could I revive within me,
Her symphony and song,
To such a deep delight 'twould
        win me,
That with music loud and long,
I would build that dome in air,
That sunny dome! those caves of ice!
And all who heard should see them there,
And all should cry, Beware! Beware!
His flashing eyes, his floating hair!
Weave a circle round him thrice,
And close your eyes with holy dread,
For he on honey-dew hath fed,
And drunk the milk of Paradise.
        Samuel Taylor Coleridge 1772–1834

from The Pied Piper of Hamelin

Into the street the Piper stept,
    Smiling first a little smile,
As if he knew what magic slept
    In his quiet pipe the while;
Then, like a musical adept,
To blow the pipe his lips he wrinkled,
And green and blue his sharp eyes twinkled,
Like a candle-flame where salt is sprinkled;
And ere three shrill notes the pipe uttered,
You heard as if an army muttered;
And the muttering grew to a grumbling;
And the grumbling grew to a mighty rumbling;
And out of the houses the rats came tumbling.
Great rats, small rats, lean rats, brawny rats,
Brown rats, black rats, grey rats, tawny rats,
Grave old plodders, gay young friskers,
    Fathers, mothers, uncles, cousins,
Cocking tails and pricking whiskers,
    Families by tens and dozens,
Brothers, sisters, husbands, wives –
Followed the Piper for their lives.
From street to street he piped advancing,
And step for step they followed dancing,
Until they came to the river Weser,
    Wherein all plunged and perished!
– Save one who, stout as Julius Caesar,

Swam across and lived to carry
  (As he, the manuscript he cherished)
To Rat-land home his commentary:
Which was, "At the first shrill notes of the pipe,
I heard a sound as of scraping tripe,
And putting apples, wondrous ripe,
Into a cider-press's gripe:
And a moving away of pickle-tub-boards,
And a leaving ajar of conserve-cupboards,
And a drawing the corks of train-oil-flasks,
And a breaking the hoops of butter-casks;
And it seemed as if a voice
  (Sweeter far than by harp or by psaltery
Is breathed) called out, 'Oh rats, rejoice!
  The world is grown to one vast drysaltery!
So munch on, crunch on, take your nuncheon,
Breakfast, supper, dinner, luncheon!'
And just as a bulky sugar-puncheon,
All ready staved, like a great sun shone
Glorious scarce an inch before me,
Just as methought it said, 'Come, bore me!'
– I found the Weser rolling o'er me."

Robert Browning 1812–1889

La Belle Dame Sans Merci

O what can ail thee Knight at arms,
　Alone and palely loitering?
The sedge has withered from the Lake,
　And no birds sing!

O what can ail thee Knight at arms,
　So haggard, and so woe begone?
The Squirrel's granary is full
　And the harvest's done.

I see a lily on thy brow
　With anguish moist and fever dew,
And on thy cheeks a fading rose
　Fast withereth too.

I met a Lady in the meads
    Full beautiful, a faery's child,
Her hair was long, her foot was light,
    And her eyes were wild.

I made a Garland for her head,
    And bracelets too, and fragrant Zone;
She look'd at me as she did love
    And made sweet moan.

I set her on my pacing steed
    And nothing else saw all day long;
For sidelong would she bend and sing
    A faery's song.

She found me roots of relish sweet
    And honey wild and manna dew;
And sure in language strange she said –
    I love thee true.

She took me to her elfin grot,
    And there she wept and sigh'd full sore;
And there I shut her wild wild eyes
    With kisses four.

And there she lulled me asleep,
    And there I dream'd, Ah Woe betide!
The latest dream I ever dreamt
    On the cold hill side.

I saw pale Kings, and Princes too,
    Pale warriors, death pale were they all;
They cried, "La Belle Dame sans Merci
    Thee hath in thrall!"

I saw their starv'd lips in the gloam
    With horrid warning gaped wide,
And I awoke, and found me here
    On the cold hill's side.

And this is why I sojourn here
    Alone and palely loitering,
Though the sedge is withered from the Lake,
    And no birds sing.

John Keats 1795 – 1821

The Lion
and the Unicorn

The lion and the unicorn
    Were fighting for the crown;
The lion beat the unicorn
    All round the town.
Some gave them white bread,
    And some gave them brown;
Some gave them plum cake,
    And sent them out of town.

Anon

The Fairies

Up the airy mountain,
Down the rushy glen,
We daren't go a-hunting,
For fear of little men;
Wee folk, good folk,
Trooping all together;
Green jacket, red cap,
And white owl's feather!

Down along the rocky shore
Some make their home,
They live on crispy pancakes
Of yellow tide-foam;
Some in the reeds
Of the black mountain-lake,
With frogs for their watch-dogs,
All night awake.

48

High on the hilltop
The old King sits;
He is now so old and grey,
He's nigh lost his wits.
With a bridge of white mist
Columbkill he crosses,
On his stately journeys
From Slieveleague to Rosses;
Or going up with music
On cold, starry nights,
To sup with the Queen
Of the gay Northern Lights.

They stole little Bridget
For seven years long;
When she came down again
Her friends were all gone.
They took her lightly back,
Between the night and the morrow,
They thought that she was fast asleep,
But she was dead with sorrow.
They have kept her ever since
Deep within the lake,
On a bed of flag-leaves,
Watching till she wake.

By the craggy hillside,
Through the mosses bare,
They have planted thorn-trees
For pleasure, here and there.
Is any man so daring
As dig them up in spite,
He shall find their sharpest thorns
In his bed at night.

Up the airy mountain,
Down the rushy glen,
We daren't go a-hunting,
For fear of little men;
Wee folk, good folk,
Trooping all together,
Green jacket, red cap,
And white owl's feather!
William Allingham 1824 — 1889

Love and Beauty

New Sights

I like to see a thing I know
Has not been seen before,
That's why I cut my apple through
To look into the core.

It's nice to think, though many an eye
Has seen the ruddy skin,
Mine is the very first to spy
The five brown pips within.

Anon

from
The Little Mermaid

Far out at sea, the water is as blue
As cornflowers, and as clear as crystal-core;
But so exceeding deep, no sea-bird's view
Can fathom it, nor men's ropes touch its floor.
Strange, snake-like trees and weeds – the same which grew
Before dry land with herbs was peopled o'er –
Still sleep in heavy peacefulness down there,
And hold their fluctuous arms towards upper air.

And it is there the Sea-King's nation dwells.
His palace, golden-bright and ruby-red,
Gleams like a crown among those velvet dells.
Pink, shimmering streams of light its windows shed,
Like waterfalls of wine; and pink-white shells,
Like Alpine snows, its lofty roof o'erspread;
Which close and open, close and open wide,
With every ebb and flowing of the tide.

Wilfred Owen 1893 – 1918

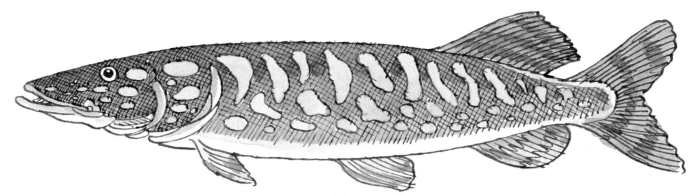

The Owl and the Pussy-Cat

The Owl and the Pussy-Cat went to sea
In a beautiful pea-green boat,
They took some honey, and plenty of money;
Wrapped up in a five-pound note.
The Owl looked up to the stars above,
And sang to a small guitar,
"O lovely Pussy, O Pussy, my love,
What a beautiful Pussy you are,
    You are,
    You are!
What a beautiful Pussy you are!"

Pussy said to the Owl, "You elegant fowl!
How charmingly sweet you sing!
O let us be married! too long we have tarried:
But what shall we do for a ring?"
They sailed away for a year and a day,
To the land where the Bong-tree grows,
And there in a wood a Piggy-wig stood,
With a ring at the end of his nose,
    His nose,
    His nose,
With a ring at the end of his nose.

"Dear Pig, are you willing to sell for one shilling
Your ring?" Said the Piggy, "I will."
So they took it away, and were married next day
By the Turkey who lives on the hill.
They dined on mince, and slices of quince,
Which they ate with a runcible spoon;
And hand in hand, on the edge of the sand,
They danced by the light of the moon,
    The moon,
    The moon,
They danced by the light of the moon.

Edward Lear 1812–1888

Romance

I will make you brooches and toys for your delight
Of bird-song at morning and star-shine at night.
I will make a palace fit for you and me,
Of green days in forests and blue days at sea.

I will make my kitchen, and you shall keep your room,
Where white flows the river and bright blows the broom,
And you shall wash your linen and keep your body white
In rainfall at morning and dewfall at night.

And this shall be for music, when no one else is near,
The fine song for singing, the rare song to hear!
That only I remember, that only you admire,
Of the broad road that stretches and the roadside fire.

Robert Louis Stevenson 1850 −1894

Lullaby –
Hush, Little Baby

Hush, little baby, don't say a word,
Papa's going to buy you a mocking bird.

If the mocking bird won't sing,
Papa's going to buy you a diamond ring.

If the diamond ring turns to brass,
Papa's going to buy you a looking-glass.

If the looking-glass gets broke,
Papa's going to buy you a billy-goat.

If that billy-goat runs away,
Papa's going to buy you another today.

Anon

She Walks in Beauty

She walks in beauty, like the night
Of cloudless climes and starry skies,
And all that's best of dark and bright
Meets in her aspect and her eyes,
Thus mellow'd to that tender light
Which heaven to gaudy day denies.

One shade the more, one ray the less
Had half impair'd the nameless grace
Which waves in every raven tress
Or softly lightens o'er her face,
Where thoughts serenely sweet express
How pure, how dear their dwelling-place.

And on that cheek and o'er that brow
So soft, so calm, yet eloquent,
The smiles that win, the tints that glow
But tell of days in goodness spent,
A mind at peace with all below,
A heart whose love is innocent.

Lord George Byron 1788 – 1824

Behold, My Brothers

In 1877, Native American Sioux leader, Tatanka Yotanka, also known as Sitting Bull, declares his love for his inherited land and his dedication to defend it.

Behold, my brothers, the spring has come;
the earth has received the embraces of the sun
and we shall soon see the results of that love!

Every seed is awakened and so has all animal life.
It is through this mysterious power that we too
have our being and we therefore yield to our
neighbours, even our animal neighbours, the same
right as ourselves, to inhabit this land.

Yet, hear me, people,
we have now to deal with another race –
small and feeble when our fathers first met them
but now great and overbearing. Strangely enough
they have a mind to till the soil. And the love
of possession is a disease with them.

These people have made many rules that
the rich may break but the poor may not.
They take tithes from the poor and weak
to support the rich who rule. They claim
this mother of ours, the earth, for their own
and fence their neighbours away; they deface
her with their buildings and their refuse.
This nation is like a spring freshet
that overruns its banks
and destroys all who are in its path.

We cannot dwell side by side. Only
seven years ago we made a treaty
by which we were assured that the buffalo
country should be left to us forever. Now
they threaten to take that away from us.
My brothers, shall we submit or shall we
say to them: "First kill me
before you take possession of my Fatherland . . ."

Sitting Bull c.1837–1890

Sympathy

I know what the caged bird feels, alas!
When the sun is bright on the upland slopes;
When the wind stirs soft through the springing grass,
And the river flows like a stream of glass;
When the first bird sings and the first bud opes,
And the faint perfume from its chalice steals –
I know what the caged bird feels!

I know why the caged bird beats his wing
Till its blood is red on the cruel bars;
For he must fly back to his perch and cling
When he fain would be on the bough a-swing;
And a pain still throbs in the old, old scars
And they pulse again with a keener sting –
I know why he beats his wing!

I know why the caged bird sings, ah me,
When his wing is bruised and his bosom sore, –
When he beats his bars and he would be free;
It is not a carol of joy or glee,
But a prayer that he sends from his heart's deep core,
But a plea, that upward to Heaven he flings –
I know why the caged bird sings!

Paul Laurence Dunbar 1872–1906

I Wandered Lonely as a Cloud

I wandered lonely as a cloud
That floats on high o'er vales and hills,
When all at once I saw a crowd,
A host of golden daffodils;
Beside the lake, beneath the trees,
Fluttering and dancing in the breeze.

Continuous as the stars that shine
And twinkle on the milky way,
They stretched in never-ending line
Along the margin of a bay:
Ten thousand saw I at a glance,
Tossing their heads in sprightly dance.

The waves beside them danced; but they
Out-did the sparkling waves in glee.
A poet could not be but gay,
In such a jocund company:
I gazed – and gazed – but little thought
What wealth the show to me had brought:

For oft, when on my couch I lie
In vacant or in pensive mood,
They flash upon that inward eye
Which is the bliss of solitude;
And then my heart with pleasure fills,
And dances with the daffodils.

William Wordsworth 1770 – 1850

from
These I Have Loved . . .

These I have loved:
       White plates and cups, clean-gleaming,
Ringed with blue lines; and feathery, faery dust;
Wet roofs, beneath the lamp-light; the strong crust
Of friendly bread; and many-tasting food;
Rainbows; and the blue bitter smoke of wood;
And radiant raindrops couching in cool flowers;
And flowers themselves, that sway through sunny hours,
Dreaming of moths that drink them under the moon;
Then, the cool kindliness of sheets, that soon
Smooth away trouble; and the rough male kiss
Of blankets; grainy wood; live hair that is
Shining and free; blue-massing clouds; the keen
Unpassioned beauty of a great machine;
The benison of hot water; furs to touch;
The good smell of old clothes; and other such –
The comfortable smell of friendly fingers,
Hair's fragrance, and the musty reek that lingers
About dead leaves and last year's ferns . . .
                Rupert Brooke 1887–1915

Laughter and Tears

I Eat My Peas With Honey

I eat my peas with honey;
I've done it all my life.
It makes the peas taste funny,
But it keeps them on the knife.

Anon

The King's Breakfast

The King asked
The Queen, and
The Queen asked
The Dairymaid:
'Could we have some butter for
The Royal slice of bread?'
The Queen asked
The Dairymaid,
The Dairymaid
Said, 'Certainly,
I'll go and tell
The cow
Now
Before she goes to bed.'
The Dairymaid
She curtsied,
And went and told
The Alderney:
'Don't forget the butter for
The Royal slice of bread.'
The Alderney
Said sleepily:
'You'd better tell
His Majesty
That many people nowadays
Like marmalade
Instead.'

The Dairymaid
Said, 'Fancy!'
And went to
Her Majesty.
She curtsied to the Queen, and
She turned a little red:
'Excuse me,
Your Majesty,
For taking of
The liberty,
But marmalade is tasty, if
It's very
Thickly
Spread.'

The Queen said
'Oh!'
And went to
His Majesty:
'Talking of the butter for
The royal slice of bread,
Many people
Think that
Marmalade
Is nicer.
Would you like to try a little
Marmalade
Instead?'

The King said,
'Bother!'
And then he said,
'Oh, deary me!'
The King sobbed, 'Oh deary me!'
And went back to bed.
'Nobody,'
He whimpered,
'Could call me
A fussy man;
I *only* want
A little bit
Of butter for
My bread!'

The Queen said,
'There, there!'
And went to
The Dairymaid.
The Dairymaid
Said, 'There, there!'
And went to the shed.
The cow said,
'There, there!'
I didn't really
Mean it;
Here's milk for his porringer.
And butter for his bread.'

The Queen took
The butter
And brought it to
His Majesty;
The King said,
'Butter, eh?'
And bounced out of bed.
'Nobody,' he said,
As he kissed her
Tenderly,
'Nobody,' he said,
As he slid down
The banisters,
'Nobody,
My darling,
Could call me
A fussy man –
BUT
*I do like a little bit of butter to
my bread!'*

A. A. Milne
1882–1956

67

Mr Nobody

I know a funny little man,
　　As quiet as a mouse,
Who does the mischief that is done
　　In everybody's house!
There's no one ever sees his face,
　　And yet we all agree
That every plate we break was cracked
　　By Mr Nobody.

'Tis he who always tears our books,
　　Who leaves the door ajar,
He pulls the buttons from our shirts,
　　And scatters pins afar;
That squeaking door will always squeak
　　For, prithee, don't you see,
We leave the oiling to be done
　　By Mr Nobody.

He puts damp wood upon the fire,
    That kettles cannot boil;
His are the feet that bring in mud,
    And all the carpets soil.
The papers always are mislaid,
    Who had them last but he?
There's not one tosses them about
    But Mr Nobody.

The finger-marks upon the door
    By none of us are made;
We never leave the blinds unclosed,
    To let the curtains fade;
The ink we never spill; the boots
    That lying round you see
Are not our boots; they all belong
    To Mr Nobody.

Anon

As I Looked Out

As I looked out on Saturday last,
A fat little pig went hurrying past,
Over his shoulder he wore a shawl,
Although it didn't seem cold at all.
I waved at him, but he didn't see,
For he never so much as looked at me.
Once again, when the moon was high,
I saw the little pig hurrying by;
Back he came at a terrible pace,
The moonlight shone on his little pink face,
And he smiled with a smile that was quite content,
But I never knew where that little pig went.

Anon

As I Was Going Out One Day

As I was going out one day
My head fell off and rolled away.
But when I saw that it was gone,
I picked it up and put it on.

And when I got into the street
A fellow cried: 'Look at your feet!'
I looked at them and sadly said:
'I've left them both asleep in bed!'

Anon

You Are Old, Father William

"You are old, Father William," the young man said,
  "And your hair has become very white;
And yet you incessantly stand on your head –
  Do you think, at your age, it is right?"

"In my youth," Father William replied to his son,
  "I feared it might injure the brain;
But, now that I'm perfectly sure I have none,
  Why, I do it again and again."

"You are old," said the youth, "as I mentioned before,
  And have grown most uncommonly fat;
Yet you turned a back-somersault in at the door –
  Pray, what is the reason of that?"

"In my youth," said the sage, as he shook his grey locks,
  "I kept all my limbs very supple
By the use of this ointment – one shilling the box –
  Allow me to sell you a couple?"

"You are old," said the youth, "and your jaws are too weak
    For anything tougher than suet;
  Yet you finished the goose, with the bones
         and the beak –
    Pray, how did you manage to do it?"

"In my youth," said his father, "I took to the law,
    And argued each case with my wife;
And the muscular strength, which it gave to my jaw,
    Has lasted the rest of my life."

"You are old," said the youth, "one would hardly suppose
    That your eye was as steady as ever;
Yet you balanced an eel on the end of your nose –
    What made you so awfully clever?"

"I have answered three questions, and that is enough,"
    Said his father. "Don't give yourself airs!
Do you think I can listen all day to such stuff?
    Be off, or I'll kick you downstairs!"
               Lewis Carroll 1832–1898

The Duck
and the Kangaroo

I

SAID the Duck to the Kangaroo,
  "Good gracious! how you hop!
Over the fields and the water too,
  As if you never would stop!
My life is a bore in this nasty pond,
And I long to go out in the world beyond!
  I wish I could hop like you!"
  Said the Duck to the Kangaroo.

II

"Please give me a ride on your back!"
  Said the Duck to the Kangaroo.
"I would sit quite still, and say nothing but 'Quack',
  The whole of the long day through!
And we'd go to the Dee, and the Jelly Bo Lee,
Over the land, and over the sea;
  Please take me a ride! O do!"
  Said the Duck to the Kangaroo.

III

Said the Kangaroo to the Duck,
  "This requires some little reflection;
    Perhaps on the whole it might bring me luck,
      And there seems but one objection,
Which is, if you'll let me speak so bold,
Your feet are unpleasantly wet and cold,
    And would probably give me the roo-
    Matiz!" said the Kangaroo.

IV

Said the Duck, "As I sat on the rocks,
  I have thought over that completely,
And I bought four pairs of worsted socks
    Which fit my web-feet neatly.
And to keep out the cold I've bought a cloak,
And every day a cigar I'll smoke,
    All to follow my own dear true
    Love of a Kangaroo!"

V

Said the Kangaroo, "I'm ready!
  All in the moonlight pale;
But to balance me well, dear Duck, sit steady!
    And quite at the end of my tail!"
So away they went with a hop and a bound,
And they hopped the whole world three times round;
    And who so happy – O who,
    As the Duck and the Kangaroo?

Edward Lear 1812–1888

O Captain! My Captain!

O Captain! my Captain! our fearful trip is done,
The ship has weather'd every rack, the prize we sought
    is won,
The port is near, the bells I hear, the people all exulting,
While follow eyes the steady keel, the vessel grim
    and daring;
  But O heart! heart! heart!
    O the bleeding drops of red!
      Where on the deck my Captain lies,
        Fallen cold and dead.

O Captain! my Captain! rise up and hear the bells;
Rise up – for you the flag is flung – for you the
    bugle trills,
For you bouquets and ribbon'd wreaths – for you the
    shores a-crowding,
  For you they call, the swaying mass, their eager
      faces turning;
    Here, Captain! dear father!
      This arm beneath your head!
      It is some dream that on the deck
      You've fallen cold and dead.

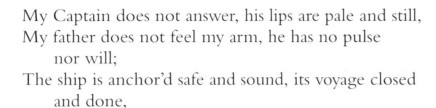

My Captain does not answer, his lips are pale and still,
My father does not feel my arm, he has no pulse
       nor will;
The ship is anchor'd safe and sound, its voyage closed
       and done,
From fearful trip the victor ship comes in with
       object won;
    Exult, O shores! and sing, O bells!
       But I, with mournful tread,
           Walk the deck my Captain lies,
              Fallen cold and dead.

Walt Whitman 1819–1892

A Birthday

My heart is like a singing bird
    Whose nest is in a watered shoot;
My heart is like an apple-tree
    Whose boughs are bent with thick-set fruit;
My heart is like a rainbow shell
    That paddles in a halcyon sea;
My heart is gladder than all these
    Because my love is come to me.

Raise me a dais of silk and down;
    Hang it with vair and purple dyes;
Carve it in doves, and pomegranates,
    And peacocks with a hundred eyes;
Work it in gold and silver grapes,
    In leaves, and silver fleur-de-lys;
Because the birthday of my life
    Is come, my love is come to me.
                Christina Rossetti 1830 – 1894

People and Places

Monday's Child

Monday's child is fair of face,
Tuesday's child is full of grace,
Wednesday's child is full of woe,
Thursday's child has far to go,
Friday's child is loving and giving,
Saturday's child works hard for a living,
But the child that is born on the Sabbath day
Is bonny, and blithe, and good, and gay.

Anon

Travel

I should like to rise and go
Where the golden apples grow;
Where below another sky
Parrot islands anchored lie,
And, watched by cockatoos and goats,
Lonely Crusoes building boats;
Where in sunshine reaching out
Eastern cities, miles about,
Are with mosque and minaret
Among sandy gardens set,
And the rich goods from near and far
Hang for sale in the bazaar;
Where the Great Wall round China goes,
And on one side the desert blows,
And with bell and voice and drum,
Cities on the other hum;

Where are forests, hot as fire,
Wide as England, tall as a spire,
Full of apes and coco-nuts
And the negro hunters' huts;
Where the knotty crocodile
Lies and blinks in the Nile,
And the red flamingo flies
Hunting fish before his eyes;

Where in jungles, near and far,
Man-devouring tigers are,
Lying close and giving ear
Lest the hunt be drawing near,
Or a comer-by be seen
Swinging in a palanquin;
Where among the desert sands
Some deserted city stands,

All its children, sweep and prince,
Grown to manhood ages since,
Not a foot in street or house,
Not a stir of child or mouse,
And when kindly falls the night,
In all the town no spark of light.
There I'll come when I'm a man
With a camel caravan;
Light a fire in the gloom
Of some dusty dining-room;
See the pictures on the walls,
Heroes, fights and festivals;
And in a corner find the toys
Of the old Egyptian boys.
Robert Louis Stevenson
1850–1894

Casabianca

The boy stood on the burning deck
   Whence all but he had fled;
The flame that lit the battle's wreck
   Shone round him o'er the dead.

The flames rolled on. He would not go
   Without his father's word;
That father faint in death below,
   His voice no longer heard.

He called aloud: "Say, father, say
   If yet my task is done!"
He knew not that the chieftain lay
   Unconscious of his son.

"Speak, father!" once again he cried,
   "If I may yet be gone!"
And but the booming shots replied,
   And fast the flames rolled on.

Upon his brow he felt their breath,
   And in his waving hair,
And looked from that lone post of death
   In still yet brave despair;

And shouted but once more aloud,
   "My father! must I stay?"
While o'er him fast through sail and shroud,
   The wreathing fires made way.

They wrapt the ship in splendour wild,
   They caught the flag on high,
And streamed above the gallant child
   Like banners in the sky.

Then came a burst of thunder-sound –
   The boy – oh! where was he?
Ask of the winds that far around
   With fragments strewed the sea,

With mast, and helm and pennon fair,
   That well had borne their part.
But the noblest thing that perished there
   Was that young faithful heart.
          Felicia Hemans 1793 –1835

From a
Railway Carriage

Faster than fairies, faster than witches,
Bridges and houses, hedges and ditches;
And charging along like troops in a battle,
All through the meadows the horses and cattle;
All of the sights of the hill and the plain
Fly as thick as driving rain;
And ever again, in the wink of an eye,
Painted stations whistle by.

Here is a child who clambers and scrambles,
All by himself and gathering brambles;
Here is a tramp who stands and gazes;
And there is the green for stringing the daisies!
Here is a cart run away in the road
Lumping along with man and load;
And here is a mill, and there is a river:
Each a glimpse and gone for ever!
                    Robert Louis Stevenson 1850–1894

The Land of Nod

From breakfast on through all the day
At home among my friends I stay;
But every night I go abroad
Afar into the Land of Nod.

All by myself I have to go,
With none to tell me what to do –
All alone beside the streams
And up the mountain-sides of dreams.

The strangest things are there for me,
Both things to eat and things to see,
And many frightening sights abroad
Till morning in the Land of Nod.

Try as I like to find the way,
I never can get back by day,
Nor can remember plain and clear
The curious music that I hear.

Robert Louis Stevenson 1850 – 1894

from
The Song of Hiawatha

Then the little Hiawatha
Learned of every bird its language,
Learned their names and all their secrets:
How they built their nests in Summer,
Where they hid themselves in Winter,
Talked with them whene'er he met them,
Called them "Hiawatha's Chickens".

Of all the beasts he learned the language,
Learned their names and all their secrets,
How the beavers built their lodges,
How the squirrels hid their acorns,
How the reindeer ran so swiftly,
Why the rabbit was so timid;
Talked with them whene'er he met them,
Called them "Hiawatha's Brothers".

Then Iagoo, the great boaster,
He the marvellous story-teller,
He the traveller and the talker,
He the friend of old Nokomis,
Made a bow for Hiawatha:
From a branch of ash he made it,
From an oak-bough made the arrows,
Tipped with flint, and winged with feathers,
And the cord he made of deer-skin.

Then he said to Hiawatha:
"Go, my son, into the forest,
Where the red deer herd together,
Kill for us a famous roebuck,
Kill for us a deer with antlers!"

Forth into the forest straightway
All alone walked Hiawatha
Proudly, with his bows and arrows;
And the birds sang round him, o'er him,
"Do not shoot us, Hiawatha!"
Sang the robin, the Opechee,
Sang the bluebird, the Owaissa,
"Do not shoot us, Hiawatha!"

Up the oak-tree, close beside him,
Sprang the squirrel, Adjidaumo,
In and out among the branches,
Coughed and chattered from the oak-tree,
Laughed, and said between his laughing,
"Do not shoot me, Hiawatha!"

And the rabbit from his pathway
Leaped aside, and at a distance
Sat erect upon his haunches,
Half in fear and half in frolic,
Saying to the little hunter,
"Do not shoot me, Hiawatha!"
            Henry Wadsworth Longfellow 1807–1882

Waltzing Matilda

Once a jolly swagman camped by a billabong
  Under the shade of a coolibah tree,
And he sang as he watched and waited till his
    billy boiled,
  'You'll come a-waltzing Matilda with me!'
Waltzing Matilda, waltzing Matilda,
  You'll come a-waltzing Matilda with me:
And he sang as he watched and waited till his
    billy boiled,
  'You'll come a-waltzing Matilda with me!'

Down came a jumbuck to drink at the billabong,
  Up jumped the swagman and grabbed him
    with glee,
And he sang as he stowed that jumbuck in his
    tucker bag,
  'You'll come a-waltzing Matilda with me!'
Waltzing Matilda, waltzing Matilda
  You'll come a-waltzing Matilda with me:
And he sang as he stowed that jumbuck in his
    tucker bag,
  'You'll come a-waltzing Matilda with me!'

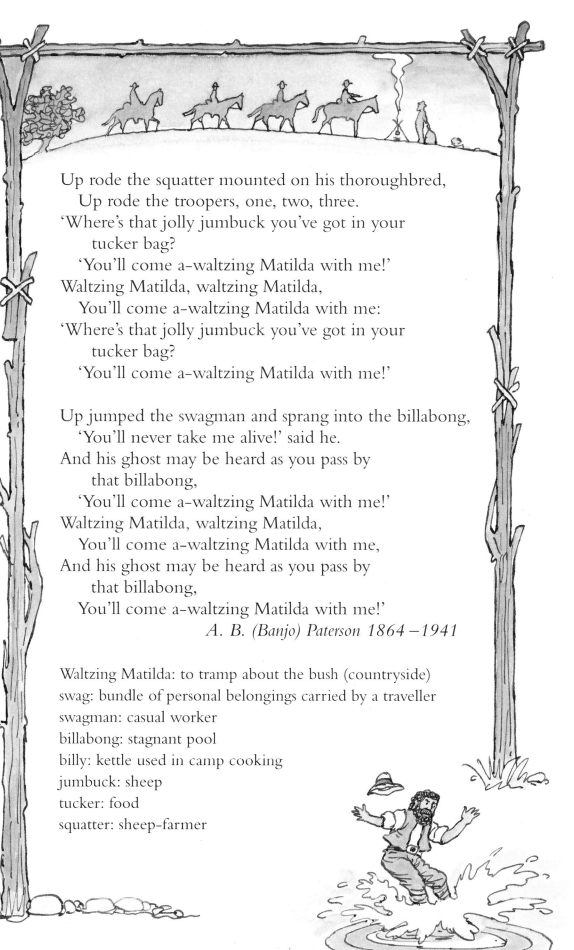

Up rode the squatter mounted on his thoroughbred,
  Up rode the troopers, one, two, three.
'Where's that jolly jumbuck you've got in your
    tucker bag?
  'You'll come a–waltzing Matilda with me!'
Waltzing Matilda, waltzing Matilda,
  You'll come a–waltzing Matilda with me:
'Where's that jolly jumbuck you've got in your
    tucker bag?
  'You'll come a–waltzing Matilda with me!'

Up jumped the swagman and sprang into the billabong,
  'You'll never take me alive!' said he.
And his ghost may be heard as you pass by
    that billabong,
  'You'll come a–waltzing Matilda with me!'
Waltzing Matilda, waltzing Matilda,
  You'll come a–waltzing Matilda with me,
And his ghost may be heard as you pass by
    that billabong,
  You'll come a–waltzing Matilda with me!'

A. B. (Banjo) Paterson 1864 –1941

Waltzing Matilda: to tramp about the bush (countryside)
swag: bundle of personal belongings carried by a traveller
swagman: casual worker
billabong: stagnant pool
billy: kettle used in camp cooking
jumbuck: sheep
tucker: food
squatter: sheep-farmer

'There was an Old Man . . .'

There was an Old Man with a beard,
Who said, 'It is just as I feared! –
  Two Owls and a Hen,
    four Larks and a Wren,
Have all built their nests in my beard!'
                    Edward Lear 1812–1888

Three
Plum Buns

Three plum buns
   To eat here at the stile
In the clover meadow,
   For we have walked a mile.

One for you, and one for me,
   And one left over:
Give it to the boy who shouts
   To scare sheep from the clover.
      Christina Rossetti 1830 – 1894

A Smuggler's Song

If you wake at midnight, and hear a horse's feet,
Don't go drawing back the blind, or looking in the street.
Them that asks no questions isn't told a lie.
Watch the wall, my darling, while the Gentlemen go by!
     Five and twenty ponies,
     Trotting through the dark –
     Brandy for the Parson,
     'Baccy for the Clerk;
     Laces for a lady, letters for a spy,
And watch the wall, my darling, while the Gentlemen
     go by!

Running round the woodlump if you chance to find
Little barrels, roped and tarred, all full of brandy-wine,
Don't you shout to come and look, nor use 'em for
     your play.
Put the brushwood back again – and they'll be gone
     next day!

If you see a stable-door setting open wide;
If you see a tired horse lying down inside;
If your mother mends a coat cut about and tore;
If the lining's wet and warm – don't you ask no more!

If you meet King George's men, dressed in blue and red,
You be careful what you say, and mindful what is said.
If they call you 'pretty maid', and chuck you 'neath the chin,
Don't you tell where no one is, nor yet where no one's been!

Knocks and footsteps round the house – whistles after dark –
You've no call for running out till the house-dogs bark.
Trusty's here, and *Pincher*'s here, and see how dumb they lie –
They don't fret to follow when the Gentlemen go by!

If you do as you've been told, 'likely there's a chance,
You'll be given a dainty doll, all the way from France,
With a cap of Valenciennes, and a velvet hood –
A present from the Gentlemen, along o' being good!
    Five and twenty ponies,
    Trotting through the dark –
    Brandy for the Parson,
    'Baccy for the Clerk.
Them that asks no questions isn't told a lie –
Watch the wall, my darling, while the Gentlemen go by!

Rudyard Kipling 1865–1936

Index by Title

Index of Authors

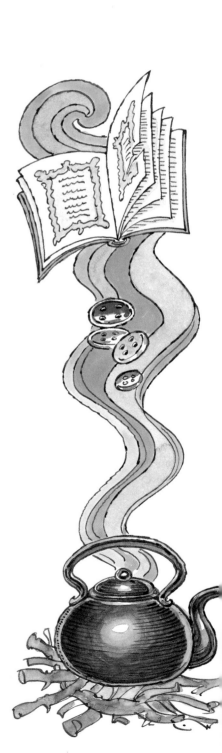